The Clarity and the Fog

poems by John Clark Vincent

Cover and interior design by Lisa D. Holmes
(Yulan Studio, yulanstudio.com)

Published in Portland, Oregon by Yulan Studio, Inc.
Printed in the United States

First edition
ISBN: 979-8-9863990-1-0

soul mate

... for lisa dianna holmes

whatever it is
that makes me love you, that makes
me need to touch you,
it works its magic on me
year after year after year.

Acknowledgements

First and foremost, I would like to acknowledge the love and support of my soulmate and partner in life, Lisa D. Holmes. She not only inspires me each and every day, she also designs and publishes my manuscripts through her graphic design and publishing firm, Yulan Studio, Inc.

I also wish to acknowledge and thank my friends and fellow writers — Waka T. Brown, Matteo Merenda, Aileen Sheedy, Linda Bybee Kapfer, and Cheryl Duffy — who took the time to read my poems (often multiple times) and provide insights and feedback which made them better.

And I'd like to thank the readers who took the time to pick up this book and open it.

Table of Contents

Section I - Poseur Sonnets

The Clarity and the Fog

There is a moment within one's lifetime
when the horizon finally clears, and
all the hope secretly held, all the guilt
secretly hid, simply comes to an end.

Each day thereafter carries us closer
to the thing we had convinced ourselves would
ever remain as it always had been...
sensed but unseen... with time yet to make good

on the myriad unkept promises
that always gave way to needs of the day.
This moment of breathtaking clarity,
wet from reality's most recent wave,

lights our way through life's encroaching fog till
our hearts, finally, can smile and be still.

Accepting Small Gifts

Loneliness, though it can become a strange
comfort to any heart in danger of
breaking, is a wholly unneeded thing.
In fact, it often serves to hide the love

which emanates from all the little things
that surround us each minute of the day.
The granite mortar that grinds the coffee.
The pert junco that comes to bathe and play.

The garden squash that works so hard to cool
the soil and shade its smaller friends as well.
Even old memories of friends who helped
fill our days now fill our hearts and compel

us to acknowledge we are not alone;
and if we are, we choose to make it so.

A Proper Goodbye

Even nostalgia ends. In time, it dies
the same death any other memory,
thought, or living thing experiences...
fading until it simply can't be seen.

Perhaps because I reimagined life,
and I strove to relive my creation
day after day until I got things right,
I prayed my dreams would come to fruition

and this mad grasp at life would allow me
to hold at least one eternal moment
of the purest joy in my heart before
life served up this last lingering lament.

But no. I can't save a thing. The best I
can do is give life a proper goodbye.

The World We See

Our thoughts matter. They blend their energy
into the ocean of life that surrounds
us. And that energy, even if it
dissipates, does not end. It knows no bounds.

It further blends itself into other
energetic waves with which it now flows.
We know what those thoughts feel like; what made them.
How they affect others, we also know.

Our thoughts are real. Knowing this enables
us to surround ourselves with true beauty;
or with anger or pain or sad despair.
The choice is ours. We choose the world we see.

And the world we see is the world we make,
day by day, with every thought we create.

Finally Letting Go

Resolving the past means letting it go.
That doesn't mean we try to forget it.
Intentionally forgetting something
takes effort. But when we let go of it,

whatsoever it may happen to be,
we set it free. If we wish to, we could
watch it drift away, or even notice
it lingering more than we thought it would.

It's like dumping a jar filled with fireflies,
which long ago had starved or died of thirst.
Clinging to them now will not bring them back.
So we watch them fall. That's what we do first.

What we do next is what matters the most.
We ask forgiveness, then we let them go.

Following the Prophet

This morning, walking through the neighborhood,
I noticed a book — *The Prophet* it said —
in the gutter near Bertie Lou's cafe.
Cover torn, filthy, it was clearly dead.

I recognized the story instantly.
I read it... hell, I revered it when I
was a kid trying to find a reason
to not just cut the cord and say goodbye

to the pain and torn dreams I called my life.
I felt then the way that book looks today.
Strangely, *The Prophet* helped me understand
I didn't have to die. Another way

was possible. Another way was free
to choose. And making that choice helped save me.

A Kindly Craft

The difference between craft and art is
the state of love created through the act
itself, regardless what that act may be.
Giving ourselves to our craft is, in fact,

the very definition of art. When
we give our whole heart to the wood or stone
or paint or poem or garden or dance,
we leave our self and step into the flow.

Knowing this, perhaps I should consider
kindness as my craft... make it my career.
I won't get published; no gallery will
display my work. I won't get paid, I fear.

But slowly, over time, I'll learn to reach
into each moment to touch, give, and teach.

Greeting an Old Friend

... for Linda

Clearly, our lives continued throughout our
absence... our time apart... since saying our
farewells then traveling in different
directions. Yet we've both made it this far.

I find that interesting. It's like we
really are two characters spending time
in the same story. Of course that's what we
are, but I couldn't see it. The whole time

we were apart, I believed our chapters
together had ended. How good it feels
to uncover a thread that was hidden...
very cool to continue this story.

It so has the makings of a good read.
Even bit parts like ours are so well said.

Section II - Wistful Waka

delicacy

lacewings are killers.
delicate; oh so refined.
they try to look meek —
too fragile to pierce a heart —
but those fuckers will bite you.

life lesson

... for caitlyn and aiden

two jam tarts for lunch.
wait, what? oh my god, so yum!
the salad can wait...
i'm like, the greens are good, sure,
but two jam tarts? uh, yes please.

the feels

this day has that feel…
it's melancholy, baby.
first day of autumn.
days two on through all will blur;
but today might leave a scar.

tough day

another case of
existential listlessness...
what is up with that?
i mean, i'm trying, okay?
it's just, like, what is the point?

first touch

my life's a ripple;
a splash — perhaps a brief surge.
the stream might notice;
not rivers nor oceans. but,
i heard the rain call my name.

treasure trove

opening our hearts
is not how we let life in.
rather, it's how we
discover life's simple gifts
patiently waiting inside.

how we learn

as i turn to look
at the memories i've made,
i see the patchwork
of joy and tears that trace life's
rich tapestry of failure.

lost creek

standing among trees...
old. fissured bark. mossy limbs.
pensive looks my way.
so many stories to tell...
can they trust me to listen?

Section III - Acrostic Reflections

Ombré

On its own, that late summer day was not particularly memorable.
More wind perhaps. I'm sure it was hot. Big sky. Feckless clouds.
But after sunset — long after, in fact — day's deep purple edge
Receded into the blackest, moonless night of my childhood.
Everywhere. That's where the stars were. Absolutely everywhere.

Moody Jazz

Maybe it's sorrow, or separation,
Or knowing you need something that's
Out there somewhere, and it's wanting you to
Decide to keep wanting it... to keep looking
Year after year. Just stay up a little longer.

Just stay awake... because it's right there.
It's oh so close you can almost feel it. Almost.
Zero hope. That's what you always end up with.
Zero hope. That's what moody jazz has given me.

Descent

Debilitated by a sudden burst of unseasonal cold,
Every Monarch butterfly migrating
South that year was forced to descend. Thousands
Clung to the Cottonwoods circling my home.
Every leaf on every tree turned orange.
Now the Monarchs, as a species, are nearly gone...
Their numbers continue to descend each year.

Fecund

Forest trail thick with leaves and wet from late autumn rain.
Each breath scented with an earthy hint of imminent decay.
Creek water, cold, moving fast, constantly rushes by.
Under the trees, sword ferns and bracken conceal the hillsides.
Nurse logs snuggle all their newborns in blankets of moss.
Damn fine weather for this Thanksgiving Day hike.

Shame

So much of our lives is spent
Holding onto the pain of
All the times we've failed to
Meet the expectations of
Everyone... including ourselves.

Ebb and Flow

Everything beautiful evolves from love,
But, strangely, life's pain also is born in the
Breath of love... but never love alone.

All manner of thoughts and desires, though
Never meant to harm, at times grow careless and
Deeply wound the ever constant soul of love itself.

For when we strive too hard or want too much,
Love is the one that suffers most. And love is the
One that must wait out these storms and calm the
Waters washing us away. Only love can save us.